COUNTRY MUSIC

COUNTRY MUSIC

BY
THOMAS A. HILL

← A FIRST BOOK →

FRANKLIN WATTS
NEW YORK | LONDON
1978

Cover design by Michael Horen

Photographs courtesy of:

RCA Records: pp. 9, 10, 22 (top right and bottom), 32 (top left and bottom), 35 (left), 56 (right), and 60 (top right); *Country Music Magazine:* pp. 22 (top left), 35 (right), 49 (bottom), 52, 56 (left), 63 (left), and 70 *Country Music Magazine*/MCA Records: pp. 60 (top left and bottom right), 63 (bottom right), and 65. /Capitol Records: pp. 14 (top left and top right), 55, and 63 (top right). /Columbia Records: pp. 29 and 46. /Chappell Music Co.: p. 14 (bottom). /Mercury Records: p. 25. /Decca Records: p. 26. /Warner Bros: p. 32 (right). /Monument Records: p. 42 (right). /CBS-TV: p. 45. /Vanguard Records: p. 49 (top); United Press International: p. 19; CBS Records: pp. 38, 42 (left), and 60 (bottom left); Elektra/Asylum Records, photo by James Shea: p. 66; Folklore Productions: p. 69.

Library of Congress Cataloging in Publication Data

Hill, Thomas A
    Country music.

    (A First book)
    Discography: p.
    Bibliography: p.
    Includes index.
    SUMMARY: A survey of country music since its beginnings among southern mountain folk and an introduction to its "stars" past and present.
    1. Country music—United States—Juvenile literature.
[1. Country music. 2. Musicians] I. Title.
ML3930.A2H55   784   77–21067
ISBN 0–531–01405–3

CONTENTS

To the memory of George Fee,
whose friends called him Nick.
He was about as good as they get.

INTRODUCTION

Just a few years ago, if you had mentioned country music to almost any northern city dweller (back then, you would have called it "country and western"), he or she might have conjured up an image of old-fashioned, woodsy folks listening to scratchy music on ancient radios. The imagined musicians would probably have been unsophisticated country boys, or towering wranglers in spangled suits. It would have been unthinkable in those days for anyone hoping to appear sophisticated to reveal a liking for that kind of corn pone.

Today, country music has come in from the boondocks. Without looking very hard, you can find fans just about everywhere. Celebrated novelists, government officials, and opera stars have gone on the public record as country fans. And, while some of the biggest country stars have done their time on farms, on the road, or in jail, some of them are music publishers, manufacturers, even bank directors. One popular country singer and songwriter, Kris

Kristofferson, is a former Rhodes scholar. All of these people have three things in common: they play music that a lot of people love, they take a fierce pride in what they're doing, and they're doing very well.

Things certainly have changed since those bygone days when the folks were woodsy and the music was scratchy. Full, orchestral string sections dominate the sound on some current country records. The arrangements are intricate. And country music is the largest industry in one of America's most modern, cosmopolitan cities—Nashville, Tennessee.

There must be hundreds of thousands—maybe millions —who dream of making it big in country music, and for the most part they all have their eyes on the same place. A generation ago, dreamers of fame and fortune were drawn to the bright lights of New York or Hollywood. Today, it's Nashville—bright lights, fame and fortune, and all.

But just what *is* country music today? Is it only whatever's traditional, or can you slip a Moog synthesizer into the band and still call it country? What's country—and who says?

To its detractors, country music is unimaginative and repetitive. It never says anything that hasn't been said before. The emotions are primitive, and the moral values are perhaps old-fashioned. At any rate, they say, it certainly isn't good music.

To its fans, country music is the music of real people and their everyday concerns—direct, unselfish, and real. Country is natural, straight from the heart. And what on earth is supposed to be wrong with old-fashioned moral values?

It depends on whom you talk to.

It does get harder all the time to say what is country and what isn't. In 1974, the Nashville-based Country Music Association gave its coveted Female Vocalist of the Year award to an Australian woman, Olivia Newton-John. Some of its members defected to form a rival organization called the Association of Country Entertainers (ACE), dedicated to what it considers more traditional ideas about country music.

The story of where country music came from, where it is today, and how it has changed is an interesting story. It involves all kinds of people from all kinds of places. A number of them have lived every line they sing.

They may not be able to define country music for you, but they'll all tell you that they know it when they hear it.

BEGINNINGS: VOICES IN THE HILLS

1

Country music could never have been born in noisy places. It had to begin far away from the city, and here's why: a person living in the city is surrounded by places to go and people to see. There are all sorts of things to do once the daily work is done. When the whistle blows, you punch out and go home. If you want excitement, you step out for the evening. Or you invite the neighbors in and sit around playing Parcheesi, or whatever.

But imagine that the year is 1910, and you live somewhere back in the mountains of Virginia or Tennessee. Your work is directly related to whether you stay alive or not. You grow what you eat, and you're used to providing for yourself. When it's all over for the day, you don't punch out and ride the subway home—you *are* home. And as for Parcheesi—well, you're pretty tired, and your nearest neighbor may be five miles down the road. That can be a lot of mountain road for a horse and buggy at night. So you stay fairly close to home.

This has been going on in your family for a few generations.

So what do you do for excitement? You take out the fiddle, rosin up the bow. Somebody grabs a guitar, maybe a banjo.

And you sing. You sing the songs you've learned from the people around you as you were growing up—songs that can be traced back to the British Isles, probably, since most Appalachian settlers were of English descent. You sing the good songs, the songs that you like, because those are the ones that people bother to pass on. A lot of what your music means to you lies in its familiarity.

In time, because of your geographical isolation, you're going to wind up creating and passing on a new music that reflects your way of life and is unique to your people. If there were somebody standing around trying to label this music that you play in the country, they might call it country music.

It is important to understand the importance that music has always had in the lives of country people. For one thing, it never has been much of a spectator sport. Back in the old days, people weren't very keen on taking a trip somewhere and paying money to hear someone perform. Why bother, when everyone in the family sings and plays? Annual family gatherings (around Thanksgiving or Christmas, for example) have long been more than reunions; they're music festivals as well.

This kind of thing wouldn't have gone over well in,

say, Wagner's Vienna, where the music-makers were a sort of craftsman's guild, to which the public was expected to pay respect.

So, what did this homegrown music sound like?

The instruments first associated with country music were those that one might learn to play reasonably well with a minimum of coaching. Time was at a premium and music schools were few and far between. The visual aspect—having your fingers do things that made sense to the eye (which might take awhile on a trumpet)—probably had something to do with the early popularity of stringed instruments: fiddles, dulcimers, banjos, mandolins, and their various relations.

One thing mountain music has not boasted until the relatively recent past is a professional arena. The operatic tenors of the world might have been training strenuously for years and then performing to thunderous applause, but nobody was doing much of that back in the country. Again, why pay somebody to sing for you when you can always sing for yourself, and for free?

There was a lot of country music going around, but very little being sold.

We're talking now about the early part of this century, back before the radio and the automobile came along. These two inventions changed country music just as they changed nearly everything else.

With the coming of radios and automobiles, two things happened. Radio station managers, confronted with all these hours of air time to fill, saw in music something that the folks might tune in. Local talent was scrounged and thrust up in front of the microphones. Performers who showed promise might be thrust up there again.

Soon there were regularly scheduled programs featuring homegrown music, and people began to gather around their radios and listen.

It was suddenly possible for performers to develop reputations.

Not only that, but if people liked what they heard on the radio, they might climb into their automobiles and drive over to hear their favorite performers in concert.

Careers were born.

In 1925, Nashville radio station WSM began broadcasting live performances of country music. These shows were syndicated to other radio stations around the country. Within a few short years, country music had a national audience.

By the late 1920s, more than a few people who had grown up singing without thinking of music as a career were beginning to attract local followings. Georgia's Fiddlin' John Carson, Tennessee's Uncle Dave Macon, Texas's Vernon Dalhart, Tennessee's Sam McGee and countless others were getting attention in the southeastern United States. The still-young northern recording industry began sending scouts down there to find out what was going on. Who were Samantha Bumgarner and Clayton McMichen, and what did they do?

The scouts returned with recordings of music that was

unlike anything being heard up North. Soon, the better performers started finding themselves in recording studios, making records for two separate audiences: people much like their friends and neighbors, who had been listening all their lives, and armchair folklorists up North, who hadn't.

Commercial country music really started getting serious with the national reputation developed by A. P. Carter and his family, a tightly-knit clan of singers and songwriters from Virginia.

Comprised originally of A. P. Carter, his wife Sara, and Sara's first-cousin Maybelle, the Carter family was so close-knit that they continued to sing together for several years after A. P. and Sara were divorced in 1936. All fine musicians, they were responsible for making popular some of the first country classics, such as *Will the Circle Be Unbroken?*, *Keep on the Sunny Side,* and their most popular tune, *Wildwood Flower.*

Due in large part to their performances on WSM's Grand Ole Opry radio program, the Carters were probably the first country performers of national stature.

There are still Carters around, too. Although the original family group disbanded in 1943, and A. P. died in 1960, Mother Maybelle is still active, touring with Johnny Cash and her four daughters. One of them, June, is married to Cash.

The Carter Family

The first true "idol" of country music was Jimmie Rodgers. Born in 1897 in Meridian, Mississippi, he grew up listening to the work songs and field hollers of black farmhands. Their music had a pronounced influence on the music he made famous.

After working as a cowboy while still a teenager, Rodgers was a brakeman on the railroads until poor health forced him to give that up. All the while, he was singing for just about anyone who would listen. He sang the old songs as well as some new ones that he was starting to write himself.

When he couldn't work on the railroads anymore, he decided to try a career in country music, and "the Singing Brakeman" was on his way.

Jimmie Rodgers recorded hundreds of songs during his short career, but the tuberculosis that had forced him off the railroads finally caught up with him, and he died in 1933 at the age of thirty-five. He was still doing sessions within days of his death, recording from a cot.

During the 1930s, country music underwent a rapid change. A lot of country music fans had cars by then, enabling them to spend their spare time wherever they wanted to. They took to hanging out in roadhouses, or "honkytonks," and they wanted to do more than hang out. They

Jimmie Rodgers (left)

wanted to dance. And a room full of dancers can make quite a bit of noise.

The whole concept of what an audience was began to change; it was no longer a group of people who came to sit and listen. The audience was a challenge in the honky-tonks. Any musician hoping to be heard had to make as much noise or more.

Suddenly you had to have a beat, and so it has been ever since.

The idea of dancing to country music wasn't entirely new, but the idea of audience as competition was. And so was the idea of amplification—electric instruments.

People back in the hills had long been playing an instrument called the steel guitar—sometimes just called a Dobro, which was really a brand name—for quite a while. It was played differently than the regular flat-top guitar; rather than pressing the strings against the fingerboard, the steel guitar player slid a steel bar up and down the neck along the strings, making a fluid, flexible sound.

When the electric pedal steel came along during the 1930s—and a strange beast it was, bearing little resemblance to what most people thought a guitar looked like— the country musicians noticed that it handled similarly to the acoustic steel guitar. And it made a lot more noise.

The honky-tonk bands needed help, so they brought in drums and electric pedal steels. *Now* they could be heard. And when Appalachian music collided with cowboy music by way of the electric pedal steel, the bands were soon playing what would come to be known as "western swing," or "country swing."

Until recently, western swing has been largely neglected by musicologists studying our roots. This is a shame, because it really is a remarkable music, blending elements of jazz, blues, hillbilly, and what was known as the Hawaiian or Polynesian sound. The musicianship of its leading proponents was sometimes outstanding.

Probably the most prominent western swing band of the 1930s was Bob Wills and His Texas Playboys. They remain the swing band against which others are measured; their biggest hit was *San Antonio Rose*.

Wills was a durable and flashy fiddler who retired during the 1960s, coming back in 1973 to record an album called *For the Last Time* with several original members of his band. He died in 1975, and his impact on country music is enormous.

In 1939, "Red River Dave" McEnery participated in an experiment at the New York World's Fair. The experiment was called television. Red River Dave and His Swift Cowboys got up in front of the cameras and performed western swing for the multitudes, which probably made McEnery America's first television star. He got a hit record out of the exposure with his now-classic *Amelia Earhart's Last Flight*, a durable story-song which has been recorded by Dickey Lee, the Greenbriar Boys, Spanky and Our Gang, and Kinky Friedman and His Texas Jewboys. As a publicity stunt, Red River Dave once wrote fifty-two songs in twelve hours while chained

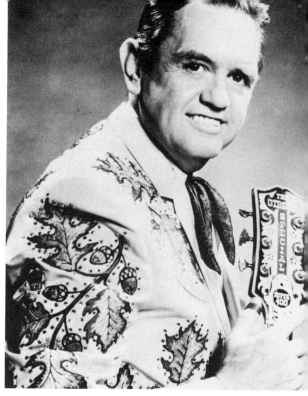

to a piano. What sets him apart from some of the other early swing musicians is that he's still at it—performing solo now but making the rounds of folk festivals and the like.

There were four "broadcast cowboys" during the 1930s with national radio shows originating in New York City: Red River Dave, Montana Slim (Wilf Carter), Texas Jim Robertson, and Elton Britt. They did much to create the market that led to the success of such people as Gene Autry, who had hits with *The Blue Canadian Rockies, Candy Kisses,* and *Back in the Saddle Again,* which would later be the theme song to his television series during the 1950s.

One of the biggest and longest-lasting stars of country and western music (as it had started to be called) was Tex Ritter, an authentic cowboy from Panola County, Texas. Born in 1907, Ritter attended the University of Texas before his way with a song and a story drew him into a musical career.

Although his recordings of *You Are My Sunshine, Blood on the Saddle,* and *Have I Told You Lately That I Love You?* made Tex Ritter a star, he is probably best remembered for a song that wasn't even authentic country and western: *High Noon,* the theme from the motion picture of the same name. That song won an Academy Award.

Kentucky's Merle Travis has contributed several classics

Above left: Bob Wills
Above right: Merle Travis
Below: Tex Ritter (left)
with Roy Acuff (right)
and Johnny Cash (center).

(15)

to country music: *I Am a Pilgrim, Dark as a Dungeon, Nine-Pound Hammer,* and *Sixteen Tons,* to name just a few. His *Divorce Me C.O.D.* was the largest-selling country record of 1946. An enduring presence, Travis is still active, showing up on television now and then and listening to "new wave" artists revive his material. The country-rock group the Byrds put *I Am a Pilgrim* on their 1968 album, *Sweetheart of the Rodeo.* John Prine recorded a hard-driving, rock version of *Nine-Pound Hammer* in 1973.

Western swing probably peaked between 1940 and 1948, as the massive population shifts brought on by World War II spread everyone's music all over. The invention of the jukebox enabled small honky-tonks that couldn't afford live bands to give their customers the latest in nationally popular country music.

With the spread of jukeboxes, country music was ready for its first genuine legend—and he was ready too.

Born in 1923 in Mount Olive, Alabama, Hank Williams was singing in church at the age of six, performing skillfully on the guitar at thirteen, and leading his first band a year after that. His career began to blossom in 1946, and Williams walked away from his first Grand Ole Opry performance a national star. That was in June of 1949, and suddenly Williams was producing several instant country classics a year. His ground-breaking songs came in a steady stream: *Hey, Good-Lookin', Jambalaya, I Saw the Light,* and *Cold, Cold, Heart* (his own favorite). Many others are still performed and recorded today, such as *I'm So Lonesome I Could*

Cry, and the timeless song that many people consider his best, *Your Cheatin' Heart.*

But if Hank Williams lived a legendary life (Cadillac, rhinestones, and all), he also died a legendary death—early, sudden, and unexpected. A lover of high times and fast living, he was a tortured and often unpredictable personality. He was twenty-nine years old in 1953 when he was found dead in the back seat of his Cadillac, which is now a popular exhibit at the Country Music Hall of Fame in Nashville.

Hank Williams was a pivotal figure in the history of country. He was the turning point, signaling the end of country's early years—the years in which it didn't quite have a solid social, musical, or commercial identity.

But, just as important, Williams represented the beginning of a new era—the era when the dream was really born. There were fortunes to be made now, legends to be carved. A large audience was eager for idols.

And so the forests, fields, and farmhouses of America teemed with dreamers—hopeful pickers who sat, strummed, and dreamed of the big time.

All they still lacked, really, was a firmer sense of unity—that, and a lot more pride.

Neither was long in coming.

MOST ROADS LEAD TO NASHVILLE

2

By 1950—thanks to radio, and such programs as *The Grand Ole Opry*, WLS/Chicago's *National Barn Dance*, WWVA's *WWVA Jamboree* out of Wheeling, West Virginia, and countless small-time variations—the national country music market was an established reality. There was no shortage of performers. Practically everybody who was anybody in country belonged to the Grand Ole Opry, which required a certain number of appearances per year and paid extremely low wages. Famous people stood in line for the privilege of playing the Opry, because it gave them even more stature and national exposure. Fans all over America would tune in eagerly, hear the new songs, and go out to buy the records. So the Opry's pay scale was unimportant. If you didn't play the Opry, you probably didn't make it in country music.

Among those making it with the help of the Grand Ole Opry was Roy Acuff, then and now considered to be the "king of country music." Born in 1903 in Maynardsville, Tennessee, Acuff brought his fiddle and mournful drawl to the

The Grand Ole Opry House in 1970.

Opry in 1937. Soaring through *Great Speckled Bird* and *The Wabash Cannonball,* he caused a minor revolution at the Opry. The emphasis had always been on instrumentals until Acuff arrived. With him, the stature of singers increased immeasurably.

Along with fellow songwriter Fred Rose, Acuff founded Acuff-Rose Music in 1942. The company has gone on to become the biggest publisher in Nashville and the fifth largest in the world.

Now in his seventies and still going strong, Acuff is a legend—conservative, traditional, and influential. His impact is impossible to avoid. Acuff comes first.

When the image of the flashy country star comes to mind, so does Webb Pierce. Wearer of rhinestones, driver of Cadillacs, singer of *Back Street Affair, I Ain't Never,* and *There Stands the Glass* (which he calls the national anthem of barroom songs), Pierce reached the height of country flashiness in the middle 1950s. He installed a guitar-shaped swimming pool in the back yard of his Nashville home, which cost around fifty thousand dollars and would probably cost twice as much now. To this day, Pierce will gladly show it to anyone who asks. He is one of the down-to-earth stars in his relations with his fans, greeting them on his lawn, selling records on the patio, and signing autographs. He receives about three thousand visitors a week at his home, and he's glad to see them.

Also flashy, but in a different style, is Hank Snow, another long-established old-timer who leans toward the cowboy image. His biggest hit was probably *I'm Movin' On* in 1950. The song has since been recorded fifty or sixty times.

Hank Thompson is best remembered for *The Wild Side of Life*. Fellow country star Kitty Wells was so angered by his declaration that wild, unfaithful women were God's curse on man that she responded with *It Wasn't God Who Made Honky-Tonk Angels*, the first national anthem of country feminists.

So country music had its national audience, but it was still an audience of country people, mostly. Those northern city folks were aware that people like Hank Williams, Tex Ritter, and Roy Acuff existed, but they didn't buy many country records. They bumped into country on the radio and on movie soundtracks, but when it came time to lay the money down, those city dollars generally wound up in the pockets of Frank Sinatra, Perry Como, and Rosemary Clooney.

In the early 1950s, "pop" music was still king, by and large, and it was also pretty dull. Pop songs kept rehashing the same old sentiments. They weren't very intense. The vocals were smooth as silk, unemotional as the freeze-dried lyrics. Pop songwriting was more a matter of grudgingly figuring out what the folks wanted than of baring the songwriter's soul. Few pop performers wrote the songs they sang.

The country songwriters, on the other hand, were often unsophisticated people who wrote just because they had to get it out. The singers tended to be writers as well, who took their songs straight to the people without straining them through performers whom they might never have met.

America was a rather prosperous place during the early 1950s. World War II had boosted the economy, and there were people who had more money than they needed. When affluent people have children, these children get some of the money—in the form of allowances, or as wages for part-time jobs.

And during those postwar years, a lot of people had a lot of children.

Nobody had ever bothered to aim music at anybody who was much under twenty-one, since young people didn't have much money to spend on records. But the war babies had money. They had different tastes than their parents and they were free to buy what they wanted.

That was when Elvis Presley came along.

It's hard to describe what Elvis Presley did. An unquestionably southern, country boy, he roared past country and became a true superstar in a category of music that didn't really exist until he came along—not as far as white people were concerned, anyway. Presley took his white, southern heritage and combined it with black, rhythm-and-blues stylings. The result, in a term coined by Cleveland disc jockey Alan Freed, was "rock 'n' roll."

Elvis Presley shook, rattled, and rolled, and young peo-

Above left: Hank Thompson
Above right: Hank Snow
Below: Elvis Presley

(23)

ple went out and bought his records by the tens of millions. They also bought some rather rowdy music by Jerry Lee Lewis, Conway Twitty, the Everly Brothers, and Marty Robbins. All at once, most of the records sold were being bought by a segment of society that had never bought many records before. And what they wanted was rock 'n' roll.

So the first country people to make it big in the northern cities did it by singing rock 'n' roll. Jerry Lee Lewis, from Ferriday, Louisiana, stormed onto the national charts with *Crazy Arms* and *Whole Lotta Shakin'*, a song that was banned on many pop radio stations that couldn't imagine what to do with it. Lewis was soon established as a major star. He sang *Shake, Rattle, and Roll* and *Great Balls of Fire*, and he didn't just sing. He played the piano, and he didn't just play it. He pounced on it, leaped and howled, whooped and jumped.

Popular music hadn't seen anything like him, and neither had country. In the early 1960s, after a few years of relative obscurity that began when he admitted to marrying a young second cousin, he was back—with a lot more country and a lot less rock. Lewis crooned his way into his second phase with such indisputably country tunes as *What Made Milwaukee Famous (Made a Loser Out of Me)*, and the country audience took him back into the fold. He doesn't rock quite like he used to, but he has developed considerable staying power.

Conway Twitty started out in Friars Point, Mississippi, as Harold Jenkins, renaming himself after the towns of Conway, Arkansas, and Twitty, Texas, because he liked the sound of

Jerry Lee Lewis

the combination. His first songs were rockers like *It's Only Make Believe* or polished ballads like *Portrait of a Fool*. But Twitty has returned to his roots in the past several years, concerning himself now with songs like *You've Never Been This Far Before, Next in Line, Hello, Darlin'*, and his successful duets with Loretta Lynn, such as *Louisiana Woman, Mississippi Man.*

Rock 'n' roll certainly came out of country, and opened up the national airwaves to country music, but not every country star who was being heard on the pop stations sang rock 'n' roll. Marty Robbins, who did start out with a weepy rock 'n' roll lament called *A White Sport Coat and a Pink Carnation*, was soon pleasing national audiences with his gunfighter ballads, such as *Cool Water, Strawberry Roan*, and the classic *El Paso*. A quiet man from Arizona, Robbins says that he wishes he'd been born earlier and could have been a cowboy. He pleased pop audiences with *Don't Worry* and *Devil Woman*, but his albums always included songs like *Big Iron* and *Ride, Cowboy, Ride*. He's almost a genre in himself.

Jimmy Dean got national attention in 1960 with *Big Bad John*, a fictionalized story-song about a coal-mining accident. He then sang *PT 109*, a song about President John F. Kennedy's World War II exploits. After the tearful *To a Sleeping Beauty*, he came out with a real foot-stomper

Conway Twitty

(27)

called *Little Black Book*. His network television show was short-lived, and he hasn't been on the pop charts recently. Still, Dean works fairly steadily.

Starting around 1960, the big-city country boom shifted into high gear. Less than eighty country stations existed in 1961, but there were over a thousand in 1976. There was a transitional period during the early sixties when the city folks were buying country records but not yet finding radio stations that specialized in country. It was during this time that the pop stations were as crowded with country music as they have ever been. "Gentleman Jim" Reeves, who had originally patterned himself closely after Hank Williams, had pop hits with *He'll Have to Go, What's He Doing in My World, Hello Four Walls,* and *Welcome to My World.*

Reeves died in a plane crash in July of 1964. Ernest Tubb, Eddy Arnold, and Marty Robbins were among the rescue party that found the wreckage.

Roger Miller burst onto the scene during the early sixties with his odd, imaginative tunes: *Do-Wacka-Do, Dang Me, You Can't Rollerskate in a Buffalo Herd,* and his most beautiful classic, *King of the Road.*

Jazz/blues great Ray Charles even got into the act for a while, releasing a version of *Georgia on My Mind* that dripped with Nashville-type strings. Charles did several

Roger Miller

(28)

songs in a country style, and they were genuine country songs, like Harlan Howard's *Busted* and Don Gibson's *I Can't Stop Loving You.*

Bobby Darin did a twangy song called *The Things in This House.*

Ray Stevens flitted back and forth between pop and country charts with novelty songs like *Harry the Hairy Ape* and outspoken social commentary like *Mister Businessman.* Long one of Nashville's most reliable studio musicians or "sidemen," Stevens is also responsible for *Everything is Beautiful, Ahab the Arab,* the first recording of Kris Kristofferson's *Sunday Morning Coming Down* and an engaging bluegrass/swing reworking of the pop classic *Misty.*

Perhaps the most obvious sign of how much country music was changing came with the success of Charley Pride, who was discovered in a Montana bar by Red Sovine in 1963. Sovine took a tape of Pride to Chet Atkins at RCA Victor in Nashville. Atkins listened and was impressed. Then Sovine showed Atkins a photograph of a black man from Sledge, Mississippi.

There had never been a black country star before, unless you count the Grand Ole Opry's DeFord Bailey, who was an Opry regular without truly becoming a star in his own right. Pride's country hits weren't long in coming, his biggest probably being *Kiss an Angel Good Mornin'.* By 1967, Pride had appeared on the Grand Ole Opry, and in 1972 the Country Music Association named him Entertainer of the Year. Today he is a director of a Dallas bank, president of a manufacturing company, and partner in three music-publishing companies. Winner of three Grammy Awards, he has sold over $20 million-worth of records for RCA Victor—more than anybody since Elvis Presley.

A remarkable thing about the established country stars is their endurance. Roy Acuff's career is but one example, as are the careers of several other stars of the sixties who were also stars during the fifties and remain stars today. Pop stars sometimes come out of nowhere and disappear just as fast, but Buck Owens, Ray Price, Porter Waggoner, Ferlin Husky, Sonny James, Roy Clark, and Eddy Arnold seem to have been around forever.

Buck Owens has had such an impact on his home base—Bakersfield, California—that it is sometimes called "Buckersfield." His biggest hits were *Tiger By the Tail* and *Act Naturally*. "Hee Haw," a nationally syndicated television show on which Owens costars with Roy Clark, started out as a network show on CBS. When CBS canceled it, its producers sold the show into syndication. "Hee Haw" went on to become one of the most popular syndicated shows in television history, appearing on over two hundred stations in 1976.

"Hee Haw's" humor is certainly corny, and most of the jokes are old ones, but it is just about the only nationally televised forum that country music has. There's a lot of the Nashville sound, too. When Grandpa Jones gets up to whoop and sing, or when Roy Clark's entire family parades onstage with their hands full of fiddles, banjos, and flat-top

guitars, you might hear some of the best old-time country around.

Eddy Arnold, known as "the Tennessee Plowboy," doesn't particularly like being categorized as country. His records are rich with lush arrangements, and he is as likely to be seen playing golf with Mickey Mantle as he is to appear at a State Fair. It has been said that Arnold, whose national hits include *Cattle Call* and *Bouquet of Roses*, could have the governorship of Tennessee anytime he wants it.

Sonny James, who calls himself "the Southern Gentleman," aspires to an urbanity similar to Arnold's, sometimes singing country music and sometimes zooming around on Nevada's Lake Tahoe in a speedboat. His first national hit was a pop song called *Young Love*, but his appearances on the pop charts haven't been frequent. Like many other "elder statesmen," he is exactly as visible as he wants to be, and he endures.

Perhaps the biggest male country star during the early 1960s was George Jones. His real-life, on-again/off-again marriage to Tammy Wynette is the stuff of which country songs are made. Best known for *Don't Stop the Music* and *Just One More*, Jones married Wynette when she was an unknown. He then watched her fame surpass his own, and the marriage ended in 1975.

Above: Charley Pride
Right: Buck Owens
Below: Eddy Arnold

If there is anyone in Nashville's recording industry with more influence than Chet Atkins, it's hard to imagine who it would be. A master guitarist who quietly releases album after album of country/pop instrumentals, Atkins is also vice-president of RCA Victor and spends a lot of time hanging around control rooms. Careers have begun on his say-so alone, and his opinion is universally respected.

Country music isn't always tears and heartache. People like Homer and Jethro are always ready to poke fun at whatever is popular or sacred.

Henry Doyle Haynes and Kenneth C. Burns started performing together during the thirties, doing goofball parodies of popular songs. Their *The Battle of Kookamonga*, a takeoff on *The Battle of New Orleans*, was a national hit during the late 1950s—probably their biggest. They released album after album crammed with parodies of *He'll Have to Go*, *Sink the Bismarck*, *My Special Angel*, *El Paso*, *I'm Movin' On*, and dozens of others. Sometimes overlooked is the fact that Haynes and Burns were legends among their peers as topflight musicians. *Playing it Straight*, an album of pop/jazz/country instrumentals that was recorded in 1961, features some rather dazzling guitar and mandolin picking. The act closed when Homer Haynes died in 1971.

The man who is generally considered to be the biggest country star of today wasn't anywhere on the scene during

Left: Chet Atkins
Right: Merle Haggard

the 1950s. Merle Haggard got a late start, and struggled for seven years to be heard, because he had spent seven of his first twenty-three years in prison. He spent his twenty-first birthday in solitary confinement, and by the time he had served three years in San Quentin prison on a burglary charge, he was fed up with jail. He went back home to Bakersfield, California, started writing songs based on his experiences, and formed a band.

It took awhile. He had a mild hit with *All My Friends Are Gonna Be Strangers* in 1965, but it was *Okie from Muskogee* that put him over the top in 1969.

The Vietnam War was raging at the time, and there was rioting in the streets of America. A staunchly conservative ballad supporting old-fashioned values, *Okie* was a strong put-down of protesters, pot-smokers, and hair-growers. Middle America loved the song, and Haggard was a star.

Okie from Muskogee, together with *The Fightin' Side of Me*, gave Haggard a reputation as somewhat of a redneck, which really isn't accurate. His philosophy of life is complex and not easily categorized. *If We Make It Through December*, a bitter, pessimistic song about recession and inflation, sold more than half a million copies in 1973, becoming a sort of anthem for the overtaxed and underprivileged. His *Irma Jackson* is a sad song about a futile interracial love affair.

Today, Haggard owns a customized $100,000 bus,

makes $15,000 in an evening, and lives in a $700,000 home in Bakersfield. His songs, such as *Mama Tried, Sing Me Back Home, Hungry Eyes, Prison Band,* and *I Take a Lot of Pride in What I Am,* have earned more than forty-five million dollars.

A close contender for Haggard's crown is gravel-voiced, craggy-faced Johnny Cash of Kingsland, Arkansas. Cash had modest hits like *Thanks a Lot* and *The Ballad of Ira Hayes* during the late 1950s, but his personal life went on the skids in 1961. The strain of two hundred ninety shows and three hundred thousand miles a year drove him to a drug habit that he says almost destroyed him. He had hits with *I Walk the Line, Ring of Fire,* and *Johnny Yuma,* the theme to a television series, but his career declined steadily until he beat drugs—with the acknowledged help of May-belle and June Carter in 1969. Within a year he had his own network television series, and a string of hit albums, including the landmark *Johnny Cash at Folsom Prison* and *Johnny Cash at San Quentin.* The hit singles came again: *Folsom Prison Blues, The Man in Black,* and Shel Silverstein's offbeat *A Boy Named Sue.*

In a classic encounter between Haggard and Cash on Cash's television show in 1970, Haggard mentioned being present at one of the many concerts that Cash has done at San Quentin. When Cash said that he didn't remember Haggard's presence at the show, Haggard said, "I was in the audience, Johnny."

Johnny Cash and June Carter Cash

Cash is married to June Carter of the timeless Carter family, and he takes the whole family with him when he tours. Johnny Cash concerts are country music family albums, with new songs, old songs, classics, and corn. He and Carter have recorded a few hits together, including *If I Were a Carpenter* and *Jackson*.

Cash is a man of old-fashioned values, but he released a troubled song about the dilemma of young people during the Vietnam War, called *What Is Truth?* And he refused Richard Nixon's request that he sing Guy Drake's *Welfare Cadillac* at the White House because he felt that the song ridicules poor people. Like Haggard, Cash is a man not easily pigeonholed.

All of these people were reaching a fairly cosmopolitan national audience during the late sixties. They had all the horns and strings they could use, but many of the songs were beginning to get a little static in their outlook: another cheatin' song, another drinkin' song, another heartbreak song. While the sound might vary from song to song, the substance was pretty much the same.

But, for better or worse, the 1960s were tumultuous years, and there were a lot of fast changes everywhere. Definitions began to fail. New attitudes took root with a speed that was sometimes frightening.

The 1960s turned a lot of things inside out, and the world of country music was no exception.

THE OUTLAWS COME TO TOWN

3

The two most significant events to hit Nashville between 1965 and 1970 may have been the arrivals of Bob Dylan and Kris Kristofferson.

In 1965, Dylan came to Nashville—long hair, radical ideas, and all—to cut an album called *Blonde on Blonde.*

No one like Dylan had hit Nashville before. Not even Jerry Lee Lewis compared to Dylan, who rounded up some of the best sidemen in town and started singing about "motorcycle black madonna two-wheel gypsy queens." He was hard to ignore.

Being Dylan, he was also quickly imitated; all sorts of outlanders began recording in Nashville. Young crazies were everywhere. The air rang with poems, prophesies, and frankness.

Country music began noticing thoughts and ideas that it had previously left alone. The sixties did that to people—forced them to look things straight in the eye.

Loretta Lynn's *Dear Uncle Sam,* a 1965 song that admitted to doubts about the Vietnam War, was quite radical for country. So were *Skip a Rope*, a Henson Cargill record that attacked hypocrisy, dishonesty, and racism. Tom T. Hall's *Harper Valley PTA*, recorded by Jeannie C. Riley, took a shot at conformity and social intimidation. Along came Johnny Cash's *What Is Truth?*

These songs squared off against complicated moral and social issues, but at least they were being sung by fairly regular types. This was your neighbor speaking, trying to make you think about something.

But while these exploratory shots were being fired, a freewheeling cleanup man at Columbia Studios—who had been in his time a Rhodes scholar with Phi Beta Kappa key, a cadet at West Point, and a helicopter pilot—was making the rounds, singing his songs for anyone who would listen, and looking for the big break (like ten thousand other people).

Kris Kristofferson wrote sarcastic songs like *The Law Is for Protection of the People*, satirical songs like *Blame It On the Stones* (the chorus of which was set to the tune of an old gospel song called *Bringing In the Sheaves*), songs with an almost mystical quality, like *Casey's Last Ride*, and tender songs like *Help Me Make It Through the Night*. But the two songs that he found easiest to sell were *Sunday Morning Coming Down* and *Me and Bobby McGee*.

Roger Miller recorded *Me and Bobby McGee* in 1969. Ray Stevens and Johnny Cash recorded *Sunday Morning Coming Down*. Both songs did well but didn't quite set the

world on fire. In fact, Kristofferson also did well without setting many fires—in the form of record sales, anyway. His hit singles have been few and far between.

So, what makes Kristofferson important? For one thing, his early songs were some of the frankest, most outspoken country songs ever recorded. They spoke of things that country music had never touched, because the touchy subjects were likely to cost a song airplay. But Kristofferson's explicit songs got airplay, and suddenly a new sense of freedom swept over the people who wrote and sang country songs. Suddenly you could speak bluntly about almost anything and get away with it. Radio stations began playing songs like *Behind Closed Doors* and *For the Good Times*, which didn't leave much to the imagination.

There had been a kind of aw-shucks quality to the way in which country music dealt with the relationships between men and women. With Kristofferson, Mickey Newbury, Charlie Rich, and others, the songs got more realistic.

This change sparked another change. If it's all right to say what you want, it's all right to think, wear, and *do* what you want.

Country musicians had previously maintained images of one kind or another—southern gentleman or well-tailored cowboy, mostly. When Kristofferson, who had looked like a

Left: Bob Dylan
Right: Kris Kristofferson

West Pointer once upon a time, grew a beard and seven pounds of hair, the standard country image began fraying at the edges.

Waylon Jennings might come to a concert looking like he hadn't slept in a week. A bearded, cowboy type named Willie Nelson, who had been around for a long time as a writer (writing *Pretty Papers* for Roy Orbison, *Crazy* for Patsy Cline, *Night Life* for Faron Young, and *Funny How Time Slips Away* for practically everybody) started generating some free-form music out of Austin, Texas. He recorded an album called *Phases and Stages* in 1974, which is generally considered to be the work that announced his arrival as a force to be reckoned with. He took to organizing enormous country music festivals every July, and the tens of thousands of people who began arriving at these affairs looked more loose-leafed every year.

Willie Nelson has become the honorary center of musical activity in Austin, Texas, which is fast becoming known as "Nashville West," a truly free-thinking country capital. Jerry Jeff Walker, the straight-shooting character who wrote *Mister Bojangles* several years before it was recorded in 1970 by the Nitty Gritty Dirt Band, revolves around Austin. So does Willis Alan Ramsey, a writer of gentle, inventive tunes like *Muskrat Love*, which has been a hit for the Captain and Tenille and the rock group America.

Waylon Jennings

(44)

People love labels, and the country nonconformers quickly became known as "outlaws." Whether Austin-based or not, they are assumed to hang together in some spiritual way.

A list of outlaws would include Tompall Glaser, who performed as one of the Glaser Brothers before going solo. Glaser is known as a real rounder, pinball wizard, and hanger-out in all-night bars.

David Allan Coe, who has spent twenty years in prison for various crimes, violent and non-violent, calls himself "the Mysterious Rhinestone Cowboy" and dresses the part. A flashy, strident individual, Coe wrote *Would You Lay With Me (In a Field of Stone)?*, which Tanya Tucker recorded, and had a hit of his own with Steve Goodman's *You Never Even Call Me By My Name* in 1975. He appeared on the cover of the *New York Times Magazine* in August of 1975—mysterious rhinestones and all.

Rock star Leon Russell, who records country music under the name Hank Wilson, may qualify as an outlaw. Michael Murphey, who won national fame with *Wildfire* and *Carolina in the Pines,* probably does. He is, to use his phrase, a "cosmic cowboy"—an outlaw with flair, partial to fancy clothes.

Texan Kinky Friedman, of Kinky Friedman and His Texas Jewboys, may walk the finest line in country. Just as there

David Allan Coe

(47)

have been few black country artists, there have been few Jews, and Friedman doesn't try to hide his heritage. With his liberal political views and Star of David-encrusted denim outfit, he can hardly be accused of striking a low profile.

There are flashy and outrageous outlaws, but there are also quiet ones—outlaws in thought, perhaps, rather than style.

Mickey Newbury is such a person. From the time he wrote *Just Dropped In,* recorded by the First Edition in 1968, he has been a steady producer of thoughtful songs like *Frisco Mabel Joy* and *She Even Woke Me Up to Say Good-Bye.*

If Willie Nelson is "king of the outlaws," his closest rival is Waylon Jennings, who has also been around for a long time. He was one of the Crickets, rocker Buddy Holly's back-up group during the 1950s. Holly, along with rock stars Richie Valens and the Big Bopper, was killed in a plane crash in 1959; Jennings would have been on that airplane if there had been room for him.

Married to country star Jessie Colter, Jennings plays the guitar in a style that he calls "chicken-picking," and has a reputation for not caring whether you like him or not.

There may be nobody in country harder to classify than John Hartford, who recorded three or four quiet albums for RCA Victor during the 1960s before Glen Campbell turned

Above: Kinky Friedman
Below: John Hartford

(48)

his *Gentle on My Mind* into an instant classic in 1968. Hartford did a couple of neo-Nashville albums then, complete with horns and strings, and appeared as a semi-regular on the television shows of the Smothers Brothers and Glen Campbell. He then stepped out of the picture for a while, reemerging in 1971 with *Aereo-Plain,* a true-grit collection of original songs backed in classic old-country style—with mandolin, fiddle, and banjo.

His commercial stature may have suffered, but not the esteem in which he is held by country diehards. On *Mark Twang,* an album released in 1976, he is the only performer —banjo-picking, fiddle-sawing, and foot-tapping his way through what must have been some mighty loose recording sessions. They also generated a fine set of classic country styles in a startlingly original mold.

What Jimmy Buffet epitomizes is hard to say. He doesn't look like an Austin outlaw so much as a Greenwich Village sandal salesman. Bearded and occasionally wild-eyed, Buffet writes songs like *The Great Filling Station Hold-Up* and *Life Is Just a Tire Swing,* but he also has a truly poetic side that he shows on *He Went to Paris.* His first album was called *A White Sport Coat and a Pink Crustacean.* He had his first national hit in 1977 with *Margaritaville.*

There are so many other fine renegades—John Prine, Steve Goodman (who wrote *City of New Orleans*), Dave Bromberg, Guy Clark (who wrote *Desperadoes Waiting for the Train,* done by Tom Rush, Jerry Jeff Walker, Tom Paxton, and others), Doug Kershaw (who wrote *Louisiana Man*), the late Gram Parsons, the late Richard Fariña, that a book could probably be written about each.

And then there is what might be called the "new wave of the mainstream"—a group of artists whose style is distinctly modern without being very radical.

Johnny Rodriguez got started in professional music when a Texas State Trooper heard him singing in a jail cell and helped him get his first job. He went on to become a respected Nashville sideman until Tom T. Hall spotted him and gave him a hand. *Pass Me By* brought him stardom.

One of the more romantic images of the day is projected by "the Silver Fox," Charlie Rich, whose suggestive ballads have had a lot to do with the liberalizing of country content. Rich had a respectable pop hit in the early sixties called *Lonely Weekends,* and then hacked around for about ten years, moving from one label to another and not causing much excitement. He broke through in 1972 with *Behind Closed Doors,* and has since established his position as a major star with *Every Time You Touch Me (I Get High)* and *The Most Beautiful Girl,* which was the most frequently performed song of 1974.

Many country stars began by writing songs for other artists. Mac Davis wrote *In the Ghetto,* which Elvis Presley recorded in 1970. Davis went on to have several hits of his own: *I Believe in Music, Baby, Don't Get Hooked on Me,* and *Rock 'n' roll, I Gave You the Best Years of My Life.*

The middle 1970s brought another mild upheaval, whose origins were primarily electronic—the trucking/CB-

(51)

radio phenomenon. Truck driver songs have been around ever since Ted Daffan's *Truck Driver's Blues* in 1940. Dave Dudley's 1963 recording of Carl Montgomery's and Earl Greene's *Six Days on the Road* is considered a classic. The song itself has been recorded countless times, by Bud Brewer, Livingston Taylor, and Taj Majal, among others.

But it took the beginnings of the energy crisis and the 55-mile-an-hour speed limit in 1973 to get America's truck drivers sufficiently concerned about police radar to outfit their rigs with shortwave radios. A subculture sprang into being: truck drivers, buddies, last of the cowboys.

They developed a CB lingo, full of slang that was bound to be incomprehensible to an outsider.

The first songwriter to feel the pulse of this mystique was C. W. McCall.

McCall was an advertising executive named Bill Fries in Omaha, Nebraska, until a local bread company needed somebody to narrate the soundtrack of a television commercial.

McCall stepped in, growled his way through a ditty that became *The Old Home Fill-'Er-Up and Keep-on-Truckin' Cafe,* and had stardom on his hands. He has since gone on cheerfully to *Wolf Creek Pass,* which describes the perils of transporting poultry across the Continental Divide, and the newest anthem in American folklore, *Convoy.*

Charlie Rich

It's also hard to know how to classify the music of Jim Stafford—"bozo country," perhaps. He has given us *My Girl Bill, Spiders and Snakes,* and *The Wildwood Weed.* He has done an album called *Not Just Another Pretty Foot.* On the cover he is shown holding a lighted cigarette between his toes. Stafford comes on somewhat in the tradition of Ray Stevens and Roger Miller, with a bit of Homer and Jethro thrown in for good measure.

Johnny Paycheck, a runaway youth from Greenfield, Ohio, sports a beard these days, but his *American Woman,* a withering rebuke of women's liberation released in 1975, identifies him with more traditional philosophies.

Glen Campbell hails from a genuine rural place named Delight, Arkansas, but the lush arrangements that back him up on *By the Time I Get to Phoenix* and *Wichita Lineman* sometimes leave country behind completely. Veteran of his own television series, his first hit was John Hartford's *Gentle on My Mind.*

The Oak Ridge Boys, whose *Rhythm Guitar* wasn't quite a hit in 1975, epitomize progressive gospel music. They come complete with beards, mustaches, and tailored bell-bottoms, and many of their songs aren't gospel songs at all. They sing with a driving rock beat and appear at the huge resort hotels in Las Vegas.

Glen Campbell

(54)

And then there is John Denver. Mention of Denver in a book on country music must cause the purists to scoff. Born H. J. Deutschendorf, Jr., and raised in the Southwest, his first national exposure was with the slickly styled Mitchell Trio, which was into the collegiate/folk bag during the early 1960s, rather than country.

Denver has contributed the recent classic *Take Me Home, Country Roads,* which was mostly written by Bill and Taffy Danoff of McLean, Virginia. The Danoffs themselves (under the name Starland Vocal Band) went on to have a country hit named *Afternoon Delight* in 1976.

Denver sings wistfully of clear skies and beautiful places in such ballads as *Rocky Mountain High, I'm Sorry, Annie's Song, Looking for Space,* and *Thank God I'm a Country Boy.*

If Denver's music must be labeled with either city or country, then it is country. But such labels don't mean much anymore.

Left: The Oak Ridge Boys
Right: John Denver

COUNTRY WOMEN: LOVE & DEFIANCE, DEPENDENCE & DOUBT

4

You may have noticed that almost everybody mentioned so far has been a man.

This isn't because women haven't played a large role in the development of country music—we'll soon see that the opposite is true—but because the role that women have come to play in country's changing world has, in itself, been one of the major changes. It should be treated separately.

Like almost any other business, country music has been a male-dominated field since its commercial beginnings. Not until 1936, when Patsy Montana's *I Want to Be a Cowboy's Sweetheart* was a hit, did a country record by a woman sell more than a million copies. As you can guess from the title, that song didn't contain any revolutionary thoughts. Safely submissive, the song became popular.

Oddly enough, though, the second hugely successful record by a woman was anything but submissive.

In 1950, Hank Thompson released a record called *The Wild Side of Life*, which says that God created wild, unfaithful women to make men miserable. Immediately, Kitty Wells shot back with *It Wasn't God Who Made Honky-Tonk Angels*, an obvious reply to Thompson's song. Each side had blamed the other in public, and the battle lines were drawn.

Kitty Wells, born Muriel Deason, is widely regarded as the first Queen of Country Music. Married to singer Johnny Wright, she was a highly successful part of Wright's show. But that's all she was—a part.

There were women having country hits during the 1950s, but they weren't doing anything very revolutionary—getting kicked around a lot and doing little to get even. Patsy Cline, who died in a 1963 plane crash, had a hit with *I Fall to Pieces*. Wanda Jackson sang successfully of *A Little Bitty Tear*. Brenda Lee released *I Want to Be Wanted*, *Break It To Me Gently*, and *I'm Sorry*.

A new group of hit-makers arrived during the 1960s with beehive hairdos firmly in place. Lynn Anderson, Dolly Parton, and Jeanne Pruett sang of heartbreak and grief. Dottie West sang for Coca-Cola.

But it was Tammy Wynette, the new queen, who spelled it out in *D-I-V-O-R-C-E*—although she could still sing *Stand By Your Man*.

Born Wynette Pugh in Tupelo, Mississippi, Tammy Wynette symbolized the country dream come true when she married George Jones at the peak of his popularity—and went on to become a star in her own right. It was a turbulent marriage that did end in divorce, but the turbulence didn't

hurt either of their careers. If anything, the resemblance between their lives and the songs they sang may well have contributed to their popularity.

There were a lot of hits, but no battle cries. Sandy Posey recorded *Born a Woman*, which said that a woman is "born to be hurt."

In 1966, Loretta Lynn came out with *Don't Come Home A-Drinkin' with Lovin' On Your Mind*, easily the most liberated song in ages. It was a declaration of independence, an assertion that no longer would a woman necessarily put up with anything a man did. Years later she created an uproar with *The Pill*, which faced the question of how many children a woman should have and who should decide.

The songs of Loretta Lynn were remarkably outspoken, and they began to turn country music around. Jeannie C. Riley recorded a sassy version of Tom T. Hall's *Harper Valley PTA*, telling everyone in a narrow-minded town just what she thought of them.

Some of the established country women had to modify their images, but the newcomers arrived with their new images already in place. Canada's Anne Murray, who first hit it big with *Snowbird* and went on to have hits with

Above left: Kitty Wells
Above right: Dolly Parton
Below left: Tammy Wynette
Below right: Loretta Lynn

(61)

Danny's Song and *I Call Your Name*, doesn't mind being photographed with her feet on the table and a beer in her hand.

Jessi Colter, who arrived on the scene in 1975 with *I'm Not Lisa*, may be married to Waylon Jennings, but she pulls her own weight.

Perhaps the most startling woman to become a star in recent years was fifteen years old when fame arrived. Her name was Tanya Tucker. Tanya was eight years old when her father decided that she was going to be a star. He traveled all over the Southwest, taking construction work anywhere that he thought he might do her career some good.

In 1973 his work paid off; Columbia Records' star producer Billy Sherrill heard a demonstration tape, and within weeks Tanya was recording *Delta Dawn*, which was her first hit. She followed up with *Satin Sheets*, *Would You Lay With Me (In a Field of Stone)?*, *Spring* and *Lizzie and the Rainman*. The superstarlet of country music seems to be here to stay.

It is probably her voice that sets Tanya Tucker apart. Husky and cool, it is nothing like the whiny drawl that some people still associate with country. It is easy to suspect that

Left: Jeannie C. Riley
Above: Jessi Colter
Below: Tanya Tucker

she could hold her own in a Manhattan hot-spot—with a change of material, perhaps, but little change in style.

What may be the most basic controversy in country music—what *is* country music?—came to a boil in 1974, when the Country Music Association gave its Female Entertainer of the Year award to Olivia Newton-John of Australia. It was indisputable that she had had the country hit of 1973 with *Let Me Be There*, which became an instant classic. She followed it with *If You Love Me, Let Me Go; I Honestly Love You; Have You Never Been Mellow;* and *Please Mister, Please*. Country audiences were certainly buying her records by the millions, but some traditionalists were alarmed. If this was country, what *wasn't* country? Did labels mean anything anymore?

When Olivia Newton-John teamed with John Denver (whose credentials as a country artist also make some people nervous) on *Fly Away* in 1975, the collaboration marked a pinnacle of sorts. It seemed to indicate that country music was just about anything that country audiences would listen to. It didn't necessarily have anything to do with Nashville or the Grand Ole Opry.

Olivia Newton-John was only the beginning of the puzzle. Is Emmylou Harris country? Is Linda Ronstadt?

Harris's sound is sometimes country, as on *If I Could Only Win Your Love*, but she had a pop-style hit with a smoky interpretation of Lennon and McCartney's *Here,*

Olivia Newton-John

There, and Everywhere, too. Furthermore, a large portion of her audience has no roots in the country at all.

Linda Ronstadt came out of the southern California pop scene of the sixties with a song called *Different Drum,* written by Mike Nesmith of the now-defunct rock group the Monkees. She became a superstar in 1974 with an album called *Heart Like a Wheel.*

Ronstadt takes old country songs like the Everly Brothers' *When Will I Be Loved?* and retools them with a driving rock beat. But her harmonies are country, and there is often a heavy dose of country instrumentation, such as the banjo on *Love Is a Rose.* Both she and Harris have appeared on Dolly Parton's syndicated television show, so they're country enough for that, anyway.

Some people have refused to accept this. Hank Snow, George Jones, Tammy Wynette, and many others deserted the Country Music Association in 1974 and formed the Association of Country Entertainers, dedicated to a more traditional approach.

It might be suspected that they're fighting a losing battle. Country music has been changing ever since it began. Pedal steel guitars were permitted. Drums were permitted. Abrasive social comments were permitted. Candor was permitted.

So what's wrong with an Australian woman who records in London?

Linda Ronstadt

(67)

TAPPING THE ROOTS

5

Is there, you ask, anybody still playing country music as it was played fifty years ago? Twenty-five years ago? Is anybody playing country that descended from the old music without being processed through Nashville at all?

They are a vanishing breed, but the real traditionalists do exist. And they are leaving their mark on a new generation of musicians, so they will never vanish completely. But the way in which their music steered around Nashville and survived anyway is interesting.

Some of them sat it out while country drifted into Nashville. They were skilled musicians who didn't try for hard-driving careers at the time.

Doc Watson, of Deep Gap, North Carolina, is one of these. Perhaps the finest acoustic flat-picker alive, Watson played small-time western swing in honky-tonks around the Smokey Mountains during the 1950s. He was perhaps ten years too young to capitalize on swing's peak years, but the swing music he heard on the radio as a child became an important part of his style.

Doc Watson

Mother Maybelle Carter

Watson was rediscovered during the folk boom of the early 1960s, and he recorded several quietly respectable albums of fairly traditional, unamplified Appalachian music. But when he got a chance in 1974 to cut a double album, he called it *Memories* and laced it liberally with country swing tunes—drums, slide guitar (unamplified this time, and played by his son Merle), and all. The album is a classic study in all of the different musical styles that Watson assimilated while developing his own.

The Carter family—minus A. P., who died in 1960—remains active. Mother Maybelle and her four daughters tour with Johnny Cash. Mother Maybelle plays more autoharp now and less guitar. Arthritis slows her down, but she is still in there strumming.

Merle Travis is still performing, as are Red River Dave and Montana Slim. Bob Wills retired in the early sixties, but he came back with several former members of his band to record an album called *For the Last Time* in 1973. Merle Haggard sat in on some of those sessions. Bob Wills died in 1975.

Turning to younger musicians who are drawing heavily on the country tradition, we find the Pure Prairie League with a song called *I'll Fix Your Flat Tire, Merle*, which describes encountering a certain country star beside the road. The Byrds went through a heavily country phase during the late sixties, when they recorded *Sweetheart of the Rodeo*. The Grateful Dead have long leaned toward a country blend. Even the Eagles, known for fairly hard-driving rock, have a strong country streak—all those high, clear harmonies, banjos, and slide guitars.

Posterity may decide that one of the more valuable things to come out of country music during the 1970s was a three-record album called *Will the Circle Be Unbroken?* put together in 1971 by the Nitty Gritty Dirt Band. Their *Buy For Me the Rain* had been a light rock hit during the late sixties.

The Dirt Band came to Nashville and persuaded Roy Acuff, Doc Watson, Merle Travis, Mother Maybelle Carter, Jimmy Martin, and Earl Scruggs to participate in a series of recording sessions. The Dirt Band served mainly as back-up for the invited guests. The result was a priceless collection of music. Some of these legendary persons met each other for the first time as a result. (A tape recorder was running as Doc Watson met Merle Travis for the first time ever; the meeting is included on the album.)

The country swing tradition lives on in groups like Asleep at the Wheel, and Commander Cody and His Lost Planet Airmen. And of course country influence is everywhere, from the jazz/blues of L. C. Robinson to the pop stylings of Wayne Newton and the rock 'n' roll of the Allman Brothers Band.

Dean Martin sings country. Nancy Sinatra sings country. Tom Jones, a Welshman who had hits with *Detroit City* and *Green, Green Grass of Home* during the sixties, sings country. Country is heard at the White House, and astronaut Wally Schirra plays a harmonica in outer space.

It may be hard to say what country music is anymore, but one thing is certain. When Richard Nixon stood on the Grand Ole Opry stage in 1974 and tried to match Roy Acuff's performance with a Yo-Yo, it signaled the end of an era. No longer does country have to struggle for sophistication. There will be no more hillbilly jokes. The world can come to the country for clues now, and if a Yo-Yo is good enough for Roy Acuff, it's good enough for a president of the United States.

SUGGESTED LISTENING

ACUFF, ROY
I Saw the Light   Hickory 125
Greatest Hits   Columbia SC—1034E
The King of Country   Hickory 4504

ANDERSON, BILL
Where Have All Our Heroes Gone?   Decca DL 75254
Peanuts   MCA 2222

ANDERSON, LYNN
Greatest Hits   Columbia KC—31641

ARNOLD, EDDY
The Best of Eddy Arnold   RCA LSP—3565
Pure Gold   RCA ANL1—1078
World Hits   2—MGM JB—5017

ASLEEP AT THE WHEEL
Texas Gold   Capitol ST—11441

ATKINS, CHET
Chet Atkins Picks His Best   RCA ANL1—0981
This is Chet Atkins   2—RCA VPS—6030

AUTRY, GENE
Gene Autry's Hall of Fame Album   Columbia CS—1035

BRITT, ELTON
Sixteen Great Country Performances ABC S744

CAMPBELL, GLEN
By the Time I Get to Phoenix   Capitol ST—2851
Bloodline   Capitol SW—11516

CARSON, FIDDLIN' JOHN
The Old Hen Cackled   Rounder 1003

THE CARTER FAMILY
Best of the Carter Family   Columbia CS—9119
'Mid the Green Fields of Virginia RCA LPM 2772

CARTER, WILF
Walls of Memory   RCA Camden CASX 2490

CASH, JOHNNY
Original Golden Hits   Sun S127
At Folsom Prison   Columbia CS 9639
The Johnny Cash Show   Columbia KC 30100
Any Old Wind that Blows   Columbia KC 32091

CLARK, GUY
Old Number One   RCA APL1—1303

CLARK, ROY
Roy Clark's Family Album   Dot DOS 26018
Entertainer of the Year   Capitol SABB 11264

CLINE, PATSY
Showcase   Decca DL 74202
Greatest Hits   MCA 12

COE, DAVID ALLAN
Penitentiary Blues   SSS 9
The Mysterious Rhinestone Cowboy   Columbia KC—32942

COLTER, JESSI
I'm Jessi Colter   Capitol ST—11363

COPAS, COWBOY
The Best of Cowboy Copas   Starday SL P 458

COUNTRY HITS
of the 40s   Capitol ST 884
of the 50s   Columbia CL 8396
of the 60s   Capitol ST 886

DAVIS, MAC
Baby, Don't Get Hooked on Me   Columbia KC—31770

DEAN, JIMMY
These Hands   RCA LSP 4618

DENVER, JOHN
Rocky Mountain High   RCA LSP—4731
Greatest Hits   RCA CPL1—0374

DUDLEY, DAVE
The Best of Dave Dudley   Mercury SR 61268

DYLAN, BOB
Blonde on Blonde   2—Columbia C2S—841
John Wesley Harding   KCS—9604
Nashville Skyline   KCS—9825

EVERLY BROTHERS
The Very Best   Warner Brothers S—1554
Golden Hits   Warner Brothers S—1471

FRIEDMAN, KINKY, AND HIS TEXAS JEWBOYS
Sold American   Vanguard VSD 79333

GENTRY, BOBBIE
Ode to Billy Joe   Capitol ST 2830
Greatest!   Capitol SKA0—381

GIBSON, DON
The Best of Don Gibson   RCA LSP 3376

HAGGARD, MERLE
Hag   Capitol ST 357
The Best of the Best   Capitol ST—11082
If We make It Through December   Capitol ST—11276

HALL, TOM T.
The Ballad of Fourty Dollars
        and His Other Great Songs   Mercury SR 61211
Greatest Hits   Mercury SR 61369

HARRIS, EMMYLOU
Pieces of the Sky   Reprise 2213

HARTFORD, JOHN
Aereo-Plain   Warner Brothers S—1916
Mark Twang   Flying Fish 020
Nobody Knows What You Do   Flying Fish 028

HORTON, JOHNNY
Greatest Hits   Columbia CL—8396

JACKSON, STONEWALL
The World of Stonewall Jackson   Columbia KG—31411

JAMES, SONNY
Biggest Hits   Capitol SM—11013

JENNINGS, WAYLON
The Best of Waylon Jennings   RCA LSP—4341
A Good-Hearted Woman   RCA LSP—4647

JONES, GEORGE
George Jones   Epic KE 31321
Let's Build a World Together   Epic KE—32113

JONES, GRANDPA
Hits from "Hee-Haw"   Monument S—18131

KERSHAW, DOUG
The Cajun Way   Warner Brothers WS—1820

KRISTOFFERSON, KRIS
Me and Bobby McGee   Monument KZ—30817
Surreal   Monument PZ—34254

LEE, BRENDA
Ten Golden Years   MCA DL 74757

LEWIS, JERRY LEE
Golden Rock Hits   Smash 67040
There Must Be More to Love Than This   Mercury SR 61323

LYNN, LORETTA
Greatest Hits   MCA 1
Coal Miner's Daughter   MCA 10

McCALL, C. W.
Wolf Creek Pass   MGM G—4989
Black Bear Road   MGM G—5008

MACON, UNCLE DAVE
Wait 'Til the Clouds Roll By   Historic 8006

MARTIN, JIMMY
Jimmy Martin   Decca 74536

MILLER, ROGER
Supersongs   Columbia KC—33472
The Best of Roger Miller   Mercury SR 61361

MILSAP, RONNIE
Night Things   RCA ALP1—1223

MONROE, BILL
The Best of Bill Monroe   2—MCA 4090

MONTANA, PATSY
Patsy Montana   Birch 1951

MURRAY, ANNE
Danny's Song   Capitol ST—11172

NELSON, WILLIE
Phases and Stages   Atlantic AT—7291
Red-Headed Stranger   Columbia KC—33482
The Best of Willie Nelson   United Artists UA LA086—G

NEWBURY, MICKEY
I Came to Hear the Music   Elektra 7E—1007

NEWTON-JOHN, OLIVIA
Let Me Be There   MCA 389
Come on Over   MCA 2186

OAK RIDGE BOYS
Sky High   Columbia KC 33057

PARTON, DOLLY
Coat of Many Colors   RCA LSP—4603

PAYCHECK, JOHNNY
Loving You Beats All I've Ever Seen   Epic KE 33354

PIERCE, WEBB
Greatest Hits   MCA DL 74999
Road Show   Decca 75280

PRESLEY, ELVIS
The Sun Sessions   RCA APM1—1675
Golden Records   RCA LSP—1707E

PRICE, RAY
All-Time Greatest Hits   Columbia KG 31364
The Other Woman   Columbia CS 9182

PRIDE, CHARLEY
Charley Pride in Person   RCA LSP—4094
The Best of Charley Pride   RCA LSP—4223

PRINE, JOHN
Sweet Revenge   Atlantic 7274
Common Sense   Atlantic 18127

PRUETT, JEANNE
Love Me   MCA 503

REEVES, JIM
He'll Have to Go & Other Favorites   RCA LSP—2223
Jim Reeves on Stage   RCA LSP—4062
A Touch of Velvet   RCA LSP—3376

RICH, CHARLIE
Greatest Hits   RCA APL1—0857
The World of Charlie Rich   RCA APL1—1242

RILEY, JEANNIE C.
Harper Valley P.T.A.   Plantation 1
Greatest Hits   Plantation 13

RITTER, TEX
Hillbilly Heaven   Capitol ST–1623
An American Legend   Capitol SKC–11241

ROBBINS, MARTY
Gunfighter Ballads & Trail Songs   Columbia CS–8158
All-Time Greatest Hits   Columbia KG–31361

RODGERS, JIMMIE
This is Jimmie Rodgers   RCA UPS–6091
Country Music Hall of Fame   RCA LPM–2531
Train Whistle Blues   RCA LPM–1640
My Time Ain't Long   RCA LPM–2865

RODRIGUEZ, JOHNNY
Introducing Johnny Rodriguez   Mercury SR 61378

ROGERS, ROY
Take a Little Love (And Pass It On)   Capitol ST 629

RONSTADT, LINDA
Heart Like a Wheel   Capitol ST–11358

SCRUGGS, EARL
Flatt & Scruggs' Greatest Hits   Columbia CS 9370
I Saw the Light   Columbia KC–31354

SNOW, HANK
Souvenirs   RCA LSP–2285
Grand Ole Opry Favorites   RCA APL1–0162
Hank Snow Sings Jimmie Rodgers   RCA LSP–4306

STAFFORD, JIM
Not Just Another Pretty Foot   MGM G—4984

THOMPSON, HANK
The Best of Hank Thompson   Capitol DT—1878

TRAVIS, MERLE
The Best of Merle Travis   Capitol SM—2662

TUCKER, TANYA
Delta Dawn   Columbia KC—31742
Greatest Hits   Columbia KC—33355

TWITTY, CONWAY
The High Priest of Country   MGM S—3849
Greatest Hits   MCA 2144

WAGGONER, PORTER
The Best of Porter Waggoner   RCA LSP—3560
Just Between You and Me (w/Parton)   RCA LSP—3926

WATSON, DOC
Ballads from Deep Gap   Vanguard VSD—S6576
Good Deal   Vanguard VSD—79276
Memories   United Artists UA—LA423—H2

WELLS, KITTY
Singing 'Em Country   Decca DL 75221
Greatest Hits   MCA 121

WILLIAMS, HANK
The Very Best of Hank Williams   MGM SE—4168
Greatest Hits   MGM S—3918
Twenty-Four Great Hits   2—MGM S—4755

WILLIAMS, HANK, JR.
Fourteen Greatest Hits   MGM 5020

WILLS, BOB
The Best of Bob Wills   2—MCA 4092
For the Last Time   2—UA LA216—J
With Asleep at the Wheel   2—Epic BG—33782

WYNETTE, TAMMY
First Songs of the First Lady   Epic KEG—30358
Greatest Hits   Epic BN—26486
We Got Together (with George Jones)   Epic E—30802

SUGGESTED READING

Cornfield, Robert, and Marshall Fallwell, Jr. *Just Country: Country People, Stories, Music.* New York: McGraw-Hill, 1976.

Gentry, Linnell. *A History of Country, Western, and Gospel Music.* Nashville: Claremont Corp., 1969.

Hemphill, Paul. *The Nashville Sound: Bright Lights and Country Music.* New York: Simon and Schuster, 1970.

Horstman, Dorothy. *Sing Your Heart Out, Country Boy.* New York: E. P. Dutton, 1975.

McCabe, Peter, and Raeanne Rubenstein. *Honky Tonk Heroes.* New York: Harper and Row, 1975.

Malone, Bill C. *Country Music U.S.A.* Austin: University of Texas Press, 1968.

Marks, Edward B. *They All Sang.* New York: Viking Press, 1934.

Neese, Chuck. *The 1972 Country Music Who's Who.* New York: Record World Publishing, 1972.

Rodgers, Carrie. *My Husband, Jimmie Rodgers.* San Antonio: Southern Literary Institute, 1935.

Shelton, Robert, and Burl Goldblatt. *The Country Music Story.* New York: Arlington House, 1971.

Stambler, Irwin, and Grelun Landon. *Encyclopedia of Folk, Country, and Western Music.* New York: St. Martin's Press, 1969.

Stoutamire, Albert. *Music of the Old South: Colony to Confederacy.* Cranbury, N.J.: Fairleigh Dickinson, 1972.

INDEX

ABOUT THE AUTHOR

A native of Chicago, Thomas Hill received his B.A. in Philosophy at Shimer College in Mt. Carroll, Illinois. He is the author of *The Guitar: Introduction to the Instrument* and *The Drum: Introduction to the Instrument,* both published by Franklin Watts.

A guitarist, singer, and songwriter, Tom recorded an album named *Ingredients* for Mercury Records in 1968 and is the composer of the song *Rhythm Guitar,* which was judged best Amateur Country Song at the 1974 American Song Festival. The song was recorded by Johnny Paycheck, the Oak Ridge Boys, and Molly Bee.

Tom now lives with his wife Vicky in a nineteenth-century farmhouse in Hubbardton, Vermont, where he works as a musician, free-lance writer, and carpenter.